𝔉ranklin 𝔇elano 𝔕oosevelt

⚜

𝔐emorial 𝔄ddress

DELIVERED BEFORE THE JOINT
MEETING OF THE TWO HOUSES
OF CONGRESS AS A TRIBUTE OF
RESPECT *to the* LATE PRESIDENT
OF THE UNITED STATES

BY

Hon. JOHN GILBERT WINANT

𝔥all of the 𝔥ouse of 𝔕epresentatives

JULY 1, 1946

GOVERNMENT PRINTING OFFICE
WASHINGTON
1948

By the President of the United States of America

A Proclamation

To the People of the United States:

It has pleased God in His infinite wisdom to take from us the immortal spirit of

Franklin Delano Roosevelt

the Thirty-second President of the United States.

The leader of his people in a great war, he lived to see the assurance of the victory but not to share it. He lived to see the first foundations of the free and peaceful world to which his life was dedicated, but not to enter on that world himself.

His fellow countrymen will sorely miss his fortitude and faith and courage in the time to come.

The peoples of the earth who love the ways of freedom and of hope will mourn for him.

But though his voice is silent, his courage is not spent, his faith is not extinguished. The courage of great men outlives them to become the courage of their people and the peoples of the world. It lives beyond them and upholds their purposes and brings their hopes to pass.

Now, therefore, I, Harry S. Truman, President of the United States of America, do appoint Saturday next, April 14th, the day of the funeral service for the dead President, as a day of mourning and prayer throughout the United States. I earnestly recommend the people to assemble on that day in their respective places of divine worship, there to bow down in submission to the will of Almighty God and to pay out of full hearts their homage of love and reverence to the memory the great and good man whose death they mourn.

In witness whereof I have hereunto set my hand and caused the seal of the United States to be affixed.

Done at the City of Washington, the 13th day of April, in the year of our Lord, one thousand nine hundred and forty-five, and of the independence of the United States, the one hundred and sixty-ninth.

[SEAL]

By the President:
    EDW. R. STETTINIUS, JR.,
        Secretary of State.

THE WHITE HOUSE,
    Washington, April 13, 1945.

Harry Truman

Contents

House Concurrent Resolution No. 161
Seventy-ninth Congress

❦

SUBMITTED BY MR. BULWINKLE

Resolved by the House of Representatives (*the Senate concurring*), That there be compiled, printed with illustrations, and bound, as may be directed by the Joint Committee on Printing, twenty-five thousand copies of the address delivered by the Honorable John G. Winant during exercises held in memory of the late President Franklin Delano Roosevelt on July 1, 1946, including all the proceedings and the program of exercises and such other tributes to the life, character, and public services of the late President Roosevelt as the Committee on Arrangements may deem appropriate, of which eight thousand copies shall be for the use of the Senate and seventeen thousand copies for the use of the House of Representatives.

Adopted July 13, 1946.

Memorial Address
by
Hon. John Gilbert Winant

United States Representative on the
Economic and Social Council
of the United Nations

Franklin Delano Roosevelt

Mr. Speaker, Mr. President, and distinguished guests, it has been the custom of the Congress to set aside a day for appropriate exercises in commemoration of the life, character, and public services of Presidents of the United States who have died. This day has, therefore, been set aside in memory of Franklin Delano Roosevelt, thirty-second President, who took office at the gravest moment of an economic crisis which threatened the security of the Republic, who twice preserved his country, was three times reelected to its Presidency, and died in office in his country's greatest war, having lived to see the victory assured but not to share it.

The final estimate of Franklin Roosevelt's achievement will not be made by us or in this room. It will be made elsewhere, and later, and by men who will judge all of us, not him alone. What Lincoln's message of December '62 said of his listeners in this same House is true of us:

We cannot escape history. We of this Congress and this administration will be remembered in spite of ourselves. No personal significance or insignificance can spare one or another of us. The fiery trial through which we pass will light us down in honor or dishonor to the latest generation.

But though we cannot pay the final tribute which time reserves to others, we can do what later generations may not do. We can speak of Franklin Roosevelt as a living man. All of us in this room, or almost all, are men and women who knew him—men, for the most part, who served with him in government in this country's greatest war. Some of us loved him well. Some of us opposed him earnestly. Many in this room bore responsibility at his request; sat in council with him. There is not one of us here who did not watch him near or at a distance, privately or publicly, in the great trial which was his life.

Greatness in a man, as in a mountain, requires distance to be seen. The things a man has lived by take their place beside his actions in the true perspective of time, and the inner pattern of his life becomes apparent. In the long range, it is the things by which we live that are important, although the timing and circumstance play their part. This was true in the life of Franklin Roosevelt. He might have been speaking of himself, as well as of the country, when he said:

To some generations much is given; of some generations much is expected. This generation has a rendezvous with destiny.

He played a great part in great events. He was his country's President and undisputed leader at a great and decisive moment in its history. Under his Presidency, the Republic reached the position of principal importance and power among the nations of the earth which it now holds. It may be, indeed, though God forbid, that the power to which the Republic then reached was the high power of its destiny: only we, the living, can determine whether that be so.

These are the facts of history which no man disputes. But greatness does not lie in the association—even the dominating association—with great events. Events have an impersonal inertia of their own and a nation is something other than the purpose of its officers of state. Greatness lies in the man and not the times; the times reflect it only. Greatness lies in the proportion.

In Franklin Roosevelt the qualities we knew were these— we who worked with him and watched him. He loved mankind. There was no one in public life in our time who had the confidence of a greater part of the people of the earth than Franklin Roosevelt. He had their confidence not only because he believed in them as men and women, but because he expected much of them as men and women. The world to him was not composed of nations only, nor the nations of classes. He did not believe in abstractions. He believed in individual human beings. The compact, as Walt Whitman put it, was always with individuals. The decisions, whether in war or in peace, were decisions which affected the lives of individuals. The friendships, the dissensions, the agreements were individual friendships, individual dissensions, individual agreements. He loved men, but he loved them to be free, to be themselves.

He was brave. There is no man in this room—not those who saw him in the weakest moments of a frightful illness—not those who saw him in the most terrible moments of the war—there is not one of us who can say that he saw Franklin Roosevelt afraid.

He was steadfast. Once the decision had been made, he stood to it. Strong-willed and stubborn of purpose, he chose the men and framed the plans to bring to bear upon his country's enemies the full and overwhelming power of its strength, turning the first and terrible defeats to victories unprecedented in the history of war. Those who know of their own knowledge what risks he had to take, what burden of responsibility he had to bear, know how to estimate his steadfastness.

He saw the facts and faced them. Even in the brief perspective of a year we have learned how well he saw the facts of danger to his country. At a time when few men other than he, whether in positions of responsibility or not, understood the meaning of the history of our time, he understood it. We know now from the mouths and records of our enemies how well he understood. At a time when it was intellectually unpopular and politically dangerous to face the facts, he faced them. Neither the initial indifference of many among our people upon whose understanding he must have counted, nor a campaign of personal vilification in certain sections of our press, rarely equaled in any country, deterred him. He carried the distasteful burden of an unpopular awakening and brought the people, not of his own country only, but of the democratic world, to see their danger while yet there was time—how little time—to save themselves and save the world they lived in.

He dared to act. It is not always that those who have the courage to see have the courage to act on what they see. Franklin Roosevelt acted. In two great crises, one within, the other without, his acts changed history. That the confidence of the American people in themselves and in their Nation was restored and strengthened by the vigor and decisiveness of his action of 1933, all of us here know, for many have shared in that action and remember well. That Britain was saved to fight the war through by the courage and decisiveness of his action of 1940 we know also. None of us who knew of that decision and its consequences can forget it now that the war is won.

He believed. There was no American of his time who believed more deeply in America than he, and no believer in democracy who had a firmer faith in man. Freedom to him was not a word but a reality; not a sentiment to which men might aspire, but a reality they might possess. The reaffirmations of the rights of man to which he committed his administration and his country in the domestic and the foreign crises of his years as President were reaffirmations not of word but fact. They stand with the great charters of mankind.

And finally, and most important of all perhaps for us who have outlived him, he dared to hope. There was never a time in the dark years of the depression, of the black years of the war, when he lost hope. And as the end of the war drew near, and the end of his life with it, his hope grew greater, grew beyond the war, beyond the victory to peace. He dared to hope for peace, to believe in peace, and to act for peace. Young in heart himself, he always thought of his country as young also, as the New World, as the builder of new worlds of peace. Believer in man, and believer therefore in men, he thought of this Republic of ours as part of that greater republic of mankind on which alone a true peace can be rested. He never thought the labor would be easy. He never questioned— he least of all men—that differences and difficulties would arise. But neither did he cease to hope. Nor would he now.

These then were his qualities as President and foremost citizen of the United States. Brave, steadfast, one who dared to see the facts, to face them, and to act; one who believed, who hoped. Whatever verdict history writes down; this much we know who knew him—that he was a man. God give us heart and will to take this Nation as he left it—not only powerful, not only rich but young and hopeful and confident and believing and strong—God give us heart and will to take this Nation forward as he meant to take it to a new, more daring future, a new world of peace.

Memorial Service
at the
Joint Session of the Senate and
House of Representatives

The Joint Committee on Arrangements

✤

FOR THE SENATE

RICHARD B. RUSSELL, *of Georgia*
SCOTT W. LUCAS, *of Illinois*
WILLIAM F. KNOWLAND, *of California*

FOR THE HOUSE

ALFRED L. BULWINKLE, *of North Carolina*
FRANCIS E. WALTER, *of Pennsylvania*
EMILY TAFT DOUGLAS, *of Illinois*
EDITH NOURSE ROGERS, *of Massachusetts*
JAY LEFEVRE, *of New York*

Order of Arrangements

ADMISSION

The House Wing of the Capitol will remain closed on the morning of the 1st day of July 1946, until 10 o'clock a. m., to all persons except Members, officers, and employees of the Congress.

At 10 o'clock a. m. the House Wing of the Capitol will be open to those to whom invitations have been extended under the concurrent resolution of Congress and to those who hold tickets of admission issued by the Doorkeeper of the House of Representatives under the direction of the Joint Committee on Arrangements.

The United States Marine Band Orchestra, under the direction of Captain William F. Santelmann, will be in attendance at 11 o'clock a. m. in the Speaker's Lobby.

TIME OF CONVENING

The Senate and the House of Representatives will convene in their respective chambers not later than 11:30 a. m. on Monday, July 1, 1946.

RECEPTION ROOMS

The President of the United States and the members of his Cabinet will meet in the office of the Speaker of the House.

The Chief Justice and Associate Justices of the Supreme Court will meet at 11:30 a. m. in the Ways and Means Committee room in the House side of the Capitol.

The Ambassadors, Ministers, and Chargés d'Affaires will meet at 11:30 a. m. in the Committee on Appropriations room number four on the principal floor of the Capitol.

The Chief of Staff to the Commander in Chief of the Army and Navy, Chief of Staff of the Army, the Commanding General of the Army Ground Forces, the Commanding General of the Army Air Forces, the Chief of Naval Operations, the Commandant of the Marine Corps, and the Commandant of the Coast Guard will meet at 11:30 a. m. in the Ways and Means Committee room in the Capitol.

FRANKLIN DELANO ROOSEVELT

The former members of the Cabinet of the late President Roosevelt will meet in the office of the Speaker of the House.

SEATING

The guests of the Congress who have admission cards for the galleries are requested to occupy their seats before 11:45 a. m.

Representatives in Congress will occupy the seats on the east and west sides of the main aisle in the rear of the Members of the Senate.

The Senators will occupy seats in front of the Representatives on the east and west side of the main aisle and back of the President of the United States and the Members of the Cabinet and the Chief Justice and Associate Justices of the Supreme Court.

The Ambassadors, Ministers, and Chargés d'Affaires of foreign governments will occupy seats on the left of the rostrum, in section A, west.

The Governors of the several States will occupy seats on the right of the rostrum, in section A, east.

The Chief of Staff to the Commander in Chief of the Army and Navy, the Chief of Staff of the Army, the Commanding General of the Army Ground Forces, the Commanding General of the Army Air Forces, the Chief of Naval Operations, the Commandant of the Marine Corps, and the Commandant of the Coast Guard will occupy seats on the right of the rostrum, in section A, east.

The Commissioners of the District of Columbia will occupy seats on the right of the rostrum, in section A, east.

The former members of the Cabinet of the late President Roosevelt will occupy the seats assigned them.

The Members of the Committee on Arrangements will occupy the seats provided for them on the east and west sides of the main aisle.

The Chairmen of the Joint Committee on Arrangements will occupy seats to the right and left of the orator, and next to them will be the Chaplain of the Senate and the Chaplain of the House of Representatives.

The Chief Justice and Associate Justices of the Supreme Court will occupy seats on the right of the rostrum.

The President and the Members of his Cabinet will occupy seats in front of, and on the left of, the rostrum.

The President Pro Tempore of the Senate will occupy a chair to the right of the Speaker.

The Speaker of the House will preside and will occupy a seat to the left of the President Pro Tempore of the Senate.

(12)

The Secretary of the Senate and the Clerk of the House will occupy seats assigned them on the floor.

The Doorkeeper of the House of Representatives will announce the guests of honor and officials and escort them to the seats assigned them.

RETIREMENT

The Doorkeeper will escort the President of the United States and the other distinguished guests from the Hall of the House of Representatives in the following order:

The President of the United States and the Members of his Cabinet.

The Chief Justice and Associate Justices of the Supreme Court of the United States.

The Ambassadors, Ministers, and Chargés d'Affaires of foreign Governments.

The Governors of the several States.

The Chief of Staff to the Commander in Chief of the Army and Navy, the Chief of Staff of the Army, the Commanding General of the Army Ground Forces, the Commanding General of the Army Air Forces, the Chief of Naval Operations, the Commandant of the Marine Corps, and the Commandant of the Coast Guard.

The Commissioners of the District of Columbia.

The former members of the Cabinet of the late President Roosevelt.

The Joint Committee on Arrangements will escort the Orator of the Day from the Hall of the House.

Upon retirement of the invited guests, the Senate will return to its Chamber.

The House of Representatives will resume its regular session.

At the conclusion of the Memorial Services the guests in the galleries are requested to retain their seats until the President of the United States and the other guests have retired.

Progam for the Joint Session

❧

Music.................... United States Marine Band Orchestra
(11–11:30, 11:45–12).

Capt. William F. Santelmann, leader

Prelude—Guilmant.
Calm as the Night—Bohm.
Melody of Peace—Martin.
Andante Cantabile—Tchaikowsky.
Adagio Élégiaque—Wieniawski.
Largo—Handel.
Presiding officer.............. The Honorable SAM RAYBURN, Speaker of
the House of Representatives.
Invocation.................. Rev. James Shera Montgomery, D. D.,
Chaplain of the House of Representatives.

Vocal solo:
Eternal Father, Strong to Save. Mr. Robert Merrill, Metropolitan Opera
Co.

(Miss Lila Edwards at the piano)

Address.................... The Honorable John Gilbert Winant,
United States representative on the Eco-
nomic and Social Council of the United
Nations.

Vocal solo:
The Lord's Prayer........... Mr. Robert Merrill.
Taps..................... Mr. Edward L. Masters, Principal musician,
USMC.
Prayer and benediction........ Rev. Frederick Brown Harris, D. D.,
Chaplain of the United States Senate.

(15)

Memorial Service

❧

MONDAY, *July 1, 1946.*

The House met at 11:30 o'clock a. m.

The Chaplain, Rev. James Shera Montgomery, D. D., offered the following prayer:

Our Father, who art in heaven, hallowed be Thy name. Thy kingdom come. Thy will be done, on earth as it is in heaven. Give us this day our daily bread. And forgive us our trespasses, as we forgive those who trespass against us. And lead us not into temptation, but deliver us from evil. For thine is the kingdom, and the power, and the glory, for ever and ever.

Amen.

The SPEAKER of the House of Representatives presided.

The Doorkeeper announced the President pro tempore of the Senate and the Members of the United States Senate.

The Senate, preceded by its President pro tempore, its Secretary, and Sergeant at Arms, entered the Hall of the House of Representatives.

The PRESIDENT pro tempore of the Senate took the chair at the right of the Speaker, and the Members of the Senate took the seats reserved for them.

The Doorkeeper announced the following guests, who were escorted to the seats assigned to them:

The Chief Justice of the United States and the Associate Justices of the Supreme Court of the United States.

The ambassadors, ministers, and chargés d'affaires of foreign governments.

The governors of States and the Commissioners of the District of Columbia.

The Chief of Staff to the Commander in Chief of the Army and Navy, the Chief of Staff of the Army, the Commanding General of the Army Ground Forces, the Chief of Naval Operations, the Commandant of the Marine Corps, and the Commandant of the Coast Guard.

The members of the President's Cabinet.

The members of the Cabinet of the late President Roosevelt.

The Honorable John G. Winant.

Mrs. Franklin Delano Roosevelt and members of the late President's family were escorted to the seats reserved for them in front of the Speaker's rostrum.

The Doorkeeper announced the President of the United States.

The President of the United States, accompanied by a committee of escort of Senators and Representatives, entered the Hall and took the seat reserved for him in front of the Speaker's rostrum.

The SPEAKER. The Senate and House of Representatives, in joint session, with their invited guests, are assembled to pay tribute to the memory of one of the great Presidents of our Republic—a man beloved by millions, not only in his country, but in every nation of the world. In these simple services we wish to keep in remembrance something of the life, character, and public services of Franklin Delano Roosevelt.

INVOCATION

Rev. James Shera Montgomery, D. D., the Chaplain of the House of Representatives. Let us bow our heads in a moment of devotional silence.

(There followed a moment of devotional silence.)

Almighty God, unto whom all hearts are open, all desires known, and from whom no secrets are hid, cleanse the thoughts of our hearts by the inspiration of Thy holy spirit, that we may perfectly love Thee, and worthily magnify Thy holy name, through Jesus Christ our Lord.

O Thou who are the Father of us all, in whose sight a thousand years are but as yesterday, we ponder the strange tidings of destiny, in which are mingled joy and sorrow. We pray fervently that Thy spirit may possess our souls so that no selfish passion may hinder us from knowing Thy will and no weakness from doing it.

Today we are assembled to give tribute and honor to him who strove to create a new era of brotherhood for our country and the races of earth. His was the sympathetic heart and open mind for those who are scourged by the ills of misfortune and affliction. For him the winds did not speak more swiftly to the giant oak than to the humblest human flower by the wayside. As we contemplate the humane purpose in the life of Thy servant, grant that we, renewed and cheered, may turn to our particular tasks and ever stand for the maintenance of spiritual integrity of our land; and walking with Thee, may find the ways of peace and concord. Through Jesus Christ our Lord. Amen.

Mr. Robert Merrill sang Eternal Father, Strong to Save, a favorite hymn of the late President Roosevelt.

The SPEAKER. The joint committee of the Congress has invited the Honorable John Gilbert Winant, a close friend of the late President, our former Ambassador to Great Britain, and now the United States representative on the Economic and Social Council of the United Nations, to deliver the address on this occasion. It is my privilege to present Mr. Winant.

Mr. Winant delivered the memorial address.

*   *   *   *   *

Mr. Robert Merrill sang The Lord's Prayer.

Taps was sounded by Mr. Edward L. Master, principal musician, United States Marine Corps.

The Reverend Frederick Brown Harris, D. D., Chaplain of the United States Senate, offered the following prayer and benediction:

God of the living and of the living dead, in a realm where beyond these voices and party cries there is peace and a pure plane of appraisal where the motives and deeds of men are weighed in juster scales than ours, and where the souls of the righteous are in Thy hands and belong to the undivided nation forever:

We thank Thee for the life of this servant of Thine and of humanity who led the Republic in the days of its most crucial test and that for the world's fairest hopes he was a word made flesh in a torn and tormented generation. We give Thee thanks that while others slept Thou didst give him to see clearly that the vital issue was a slave world or a free world, and that Thou didst anoint him to make our America the arsenal of democracy's weapons for imperiled freedom everywhere.

Now that that foul tyranny is in dust and ashes we come to acknowledge in this Chamber, where with failing physical strength and faltering voice he gave a last account of his stewardship, that among the shining memories of the Nation he served will abide always the heritage of his personal courage, his utter faith in democracy, and his passion to uplift the underprivileged and the exploited everywhere.

We think tenderly today of his heroic triumph over bodily affliction and disability, a precious gift he has bequeathed to all who with maimed bodies have returned from the carnage to face the test he surmounted in the art of living. This memorial hour we would listen to his parting words, his marching orders, as Commander in Chief, as, being dead, he yet speaketh:

Let us move forward with a strong and active faith, remembering that the only limit to our realization of tomorrow is our doubts of today.

We are grateful that in Thy providence before he ceased at once to live and to work he knew that triumph was perching on Allied banners, and that every white cross on far-stretching God's acres under alien skies was a belfry for the chimes of victory.

And now, under the spell of his example, with the elixir of his winged words still ours, we pray that when for us all the voices that praise or blame grow faint and drift away, Thou wilt give us to know that Thy everlasting arms are still there beneath us. At the last, when the fever of life here is over, bring us all to the homeland of Thy eternal love. In the Redeemer's name. Amen.

Now the God of peace, that brought again from the dead our Lord Jesus, that great Shepherd of the sheep, through the blood of the everlasting covenant, make you perfect in every good work to do His will, working in you that which is well pleasing in His sight, through Jesus Christ; to whom be glory forever and ever. Amen.

The SPEAKER. The joint session of the two Houses is now dissolved.

The President and his Cabinet, Mr. Winant, the members of the late President Roosevelt's Cabinet, the Diplomatic Corps, Mrs. Roosevelt and members of the late President Roosevelt's family, the Chief Justice of the United States and the Associate Justices of the Supreme Court of the United States, the governors of States and the Commissioners of the District of Columbia, the Chief of Staff to the Commander in Chief of the Army and Navy, the Chief of Staff of the Army, the commanding general of the Army Ground Forces, the

FRANKLIN DELANO ROOSEVELT

Chief of Naval Operations, the Commandant of the Marine Corps, the Commandant of the Coast Guard, the President pro tempore of the Senate and the Members of the Senate retired.

Thereupon, at 12 o'clock and 30 minutes p. m., the joint session of the two Houses was dissolved.

Proceedings
in the
United States Senate

Proceedings in the Senate

*

The Senate met in executive session at 12 o'clock meridian, on the expiration of the recess.

The Reverend Hunter M. Lewis, B. D., associate minister, Church of the Epiphany, Washington, D. C., offered the following prayer:

O Almighty God, the God of the spirits of all flesh, Author of life and Lord of death: We bow our heads in silent grief that it hast pleased Thee to call unto Thyself the soul of Thy servant, Franklin, into whose hands Thou hadst placed the leadership of our Nation.

For his stainless character, the richness of his intellect, and his unremitting service to his country in time of sorest need, we yield Thee humble thanks, O Lord, beseeching Thee to help us to pray "Thy will be done." Lord, vouchsafe him light and rest, joy and consolation in Thy presence, in the ample folds of Thy great love.

Comfort, we beseech Thee, his loved ones in their sorrow. Remember them, O Lord, in mercy; endue their souls with patience, and give them grace to know that neither death nor life can separate them from loved ones who are with Thee.

O God of our salvation, in the midst of sudden perplexity, may we find Thy peace. Grant to the President of our Nation special gifts of wisdom and understanding, of counsel and strength. Dispel for us all the night of doubt and fear, and lighten our darkness as we go forward in Thy name, until at length we, too, may hear Thy voice, "Well done, thou good and faithful servant." Through Jesus Christ our Lord. Amen.

Mr. BARKLEY. Mr. President, while the Senate has not yet received, according to custom, official notice of the death of the President of the United States, I am sure that all of us who as' semble here this morning assemble with heavy hearts and with depressed spirits. We assemble, Mr. President, in the midst of grief, not only on the part of our official body, not only on the part of the Congress, not only on the part of the American people, but we assemble amid that grief and contrition of spirit that pervades the entire world at this hour.

It is given to few men to occupy the Chief Magistracy of this great Nation of ours, which was conceived in liberty and dedi' cated, as Lincoln said, to the proposition that all men are created equal; not equal in physical power, not equal in intellectual en' dowments, not equal either in moral fiber, but without regard to differences—physical, moral, or intellectual—without regard to differences of race, color, or religion, are born equal in the right and opportunity to enjoy the blessings of freedom under a Nation and under laws and under a system which undertakes, so far as human institutions can do so, to guarantee the equal enjoyment of every right which a government ought to guar' antee to those who support and defend it. It is, therefore, given to few men to attain this high distinction as the head of a nation so dedicated and so conceived, but it is a rarer thing for fate and destiny to call to supreme leadership in the world any man born of woman. Franklin D. Roosevelt enjoyed that high distinction.

We do not honor him today merely because the American people allowed him to shatter precedent; we do not honor him merely because he, through the interposition of destiny, became a world leader; we honor him today because also of his personal qualities—of his moral and intellectual stature; we honor him as

an American; we honor him as a citizen of the world in the true
sense, and we rejoice to honor him in that capacity because
wherever men long for liberty, wherever they fight for the
enjoyment of human rights, wherever they shed their blood
today or tomorrow, or lay down their lives in order that a great
ideal may be attained, his name is and will be cherished and
revered around the world and throughout all the ages.

Born to affluence, in which so many seek repose and enjoyment, he was unwilling to live the life of the idle. Early in life
he espoused the cause of the common man and the common
woman. Early in life he dedicated his abilities which in many
respects were so amazing, to the cause of those who are inar-
ticulate, those whose names never appear in the columns of the
press, those about whom books are never written, those who
dwell in the shadows rather than on the peaks of human
existence, those who dwell in the shadows where the sun rarely
penetrates to shed that light of intellectual and moral superior-
ity which ought to be, and is, the ambition of every normal
human being.

Franklin D. Roosevelt spurned the idleness, spurned the list-
lessness, spurned the repose which might have been his for the
asking, in order that he might become here, and as an agency of
fate throughout the world, the symbol and the spokesman of all
those who hope for a better life and for a better world.

Stricken down in early life by an affliction which might also
have caused him, with justification, to look forward to a life of
inactivity and of comfortable ease, so far as man may be said
to have ease and comfort when stricken by a physical malady
from which he never wholly recovers, he was unwilling to
assume the posture of inactivity or of repose, because in that
body of his, stricken as it was by this affliction, there was an
indomitable spirit, there was a moral and intellectual strength
which would not permit him, in this great world of opportunity,

to spend the remainder of his life as many others would have been induced to spend it under such an overwhelming handicap.

We honor him today, Mr. President, not only because earlier he overcame what might have been a logical and natural tend-ency, and later overcame physical handicaps the equal of which no man in his station had ever encountered in this or any other nation, we honor him today, as we have honored him in the years gone by, because he conquered overwhelming burdens and hardships, because his moral and spiritual make-up enabled him to overcome physical handicaps, because in his case mind was supreme over matter, by reason of which he became, in my judgment, the world's greatest leader while he occupied the station of leadership.

He had great qualities, Mr. President, but he did not possess those great qualities without great faults, for God has not so designed life that men may be without faults, however great may be their intellectual and moral qualities. All great men have been possessed of faults, as well as high and noble qualities. Washington had them, Jefferson had them, Lincoln had them, Woodrow Wilson had them, Franklin D. Roosevelt had them. But in the magnitude of Franklin Roosevelt's performance, in the magnitude of his accomplishment, in the magnitude of his influence, in the magnitude of the reverence and respect and almost adoration in which he has been held throughout the world, faults are swallowed up, and will be swallowed up when the impartial historian shall write the record not only of this man, but of the time in which he lived. Faults will be swal-lowed up in the affirmative record of virtues and great success, like death itself is swallowed up in victory.

It was my good fortune to be intimately acquainted with the President. I had known him as Assistant Secretary of the Navy in the administration of Woodrow Wilson. I had known and seen him at national conventions of his political party. I had seen him at San Francisco in 1920 when he was nominated for Vice President. I had seen him in New York in 1924 as he came out upon the platform to place in nomination for the high office which he afterwards held with such distinction, and from which he has just departed, that Happy Warrior who preceded him to the grave by only a few months. I saw him again at Houston, Tex., 4 years later, when, somewhat improved from the physical illness from which he suffered in 1924, he again placed the same man in nomination for this high office. I saw him fly to Chicago in 1932, taking no note of danger, taking no note of chance, but coming there to inspire those who had honored him with the nomination which led to his election to a great office. I had seen much more of him during the last 12 years, in which, by reason of my official position, I came in con-stant contact with him.

I did not always agree with the President about everything. In almost every case when we had divergent views we discussed them in the utmost frankness and candor, and nearly always came to an agreement about the policy which should be adopted. But when we now and then may have disagreed, either as to policy or principle, we did so with a recognition of the sincerity of each other, of the right of each to entertain and retain and to fight for the things in which we believed. We did so with that utmost respect which I always held for him, and that affection with which I looked upon him as a person and as a President of the United States. I always had the satisfaction of feeling that I also enjoyed his respect and his affection, and he gave me assurance of both on innumerable occasions.

Mr. President, I should be utterly insincere and ungrateful if I did not here acknowledge before my colleagues and before my country that I entertained for the President, and for all he represented, the deepest affection and the deepest respect. So much so, Mr. President, that I find it difficult now, with the emotions which stir my heart, to speak upon the subject.

FRANKLIN DELANO ROOSEVELT

In the midst of our grief we must take new courage. His tired body rests in the long sleep which it has earned, worn out in the service of his country, worn out in the service of the ideals of this man who became as much a casualty of this war as any soldier, sailor, marine, or other American, or the follower of any flag, no matter upon what battlefield he may have fought, but his spirit, Mr. President, lives today, and it will continue to live and to inspire our country and to inspire the world.

In our grief let us take new courage, let us tighten our belts on this day of sadness, let us gird our loins, and, with unity, with courage, and with determination let us move forward to the attainment of the goal which he set for us not only here but throughout the world.

For the President's family I voice our inexpressible sorrow and grief. I cannot overlook or forget the stoicism, the courage, and the fortitude with which his wife accepts this visitation of Providence.

In the new President, who so lately was among us here, I express my utmost confidence, and assure him of my desire to cooperate. I believe I express the will of the Senate when I say that all of us here, without regard to politics, desire to accord to him that sympathetic cooperation which is so essential, and which he will need in the days which are to come.

Mr. President, in the light of the President's passing, in view of the sentiments which I have attempted feebly to put into words, I send to the desk, as in legislative session, a resolution which I ask the Senate to consider.

The ACTING PRESIDENT pro tempore. As in legislative session, the clerk will read the resolution.

The Chief Clerk read the resolution (S. Res. 119), as follows:

Resolved, That the Senate has learned with profound regret and sorrow of the death of the late President of the United States, Hon. Franklin Delano Roosevelt, illustrious statesman and leader in the Nation and in the world.

FRANKLIN DELANO ROOSEVELT

Resolved, That as a token of honor and in recognition of his eminent and distinguished public services to the Nation and to the world, the Presiding Officer of the Senate shall appoint a committee of 16 Senators to join a similar committee to be appointed on the part of the House of Representatives to attend the funeral services of the late President.

Resolved, That the Senate tenders its deep sympathy to the members of the family of the late President in their sad bereavement.

Resolved, That the Secretary communicate these resolutions to the House of Representatives and transmit a copy thereof to the family of the late President.

Mr. WHITE. Mr. President, within the span of my life, six Presidents of the United States have died in office or soon after the relinquishment of their official burdens. No one of them, no President since Abraham Lincoln, met the weight and complexity of problems which for 12 long years rested upon our President whose death we today sorrowfully note.

The passing of Franklin D. Roosevelt is one of history's somber tragedies. He was a great leader of our people and of world thought and effort. His genius in leadership was unmatched in the political life of our Nation. He had a vision which looked beyond the near, to new horizons, and he sought in these adventure and advance of our social, economic, and political frontiers.

Mr. President, he had a magnificent courage which lifted him above and beyond physical infirmities.

At the hour of his passing, there were bound to him in amazing degree the loyalty and affection of countless millions here and throughout the world. He rapidly and surely approached in the ending of war and his plans for a world organization of united nations, the grand climacteric of his career.

Mr. President, I am assured that great as is this country's loss, the tasks begun by President Roosevelt in behalf of victory, of justice, and of peace, will be finished, and that a better world will come. His indomitable spirit will lead in his death as he led in life.

(31)

To Mrs. Roosevelt and to her family go assurances of my deepest and my abiding sympathy.

Mr. WAGNER. Mr. President, Franklin D. Roosevelt, the greatest man New York has ever given to the Nation, as great a man as America has ever given to the world, is gone.

As Moses, who brought from God to man the old commandments at the foundation of our ethics, died after seeing but before entering the promised land into which he was leading his people out of the wilderness, so Roosevelt, the modern spokesman for social justice, the modern champion of the liberties of all peoples, has left us just short of full attainment of his goals.

But let us take comfort that God gave him more than a glimpse of the success of his work. The President knew yesterday morning that victory was in our hands. He knew that the world organization, for which he strove, had become a reality. He knew that his voice in the wilderness, warning us of the dangers of international barbarism, had become a great voice heard by all mankind.

I remember Franklin Roosevelt as a young man in the New York State Senate, back in 1911, when both he and I were Senators in that body. He showed then of what he was made. When he started a battle for progressive legislation, or for good government, he never let up until his objective was attained. In the same way, he overcame a physical catastrophy that would have made most men lose hope. As President, he began at once to work with all his courage and great gifts, for the welfare of his fellow man. Nothing could deter him. He brought health to our economy by strengthening it with social justice. His reforms will be felt for generations.

That was the first half of his work. The second half began in 1937 or even earlier, when he commenced to fight fascism with all his heart, with all his soul, and with all his might. He aroused us to our danger. He organized us for victory. Now, with Berlin almost taken, our leader is fallen.

But Roosevelt still lives, and will ever live. His wisdom and example will guide his successor, Harry S. Truman, to whom our Nation now looks with understanding and confidence and full support in the great tasks falling upon him.

May America and the world have the strength to complete what Roosevelt more than started—to complete a just and lasting peace—and then finish here in America the task of creating opportunities for all the people to earn decent livelihoods, to live in good homes, to educate their children well, and to be protected in their illness and old age.

Franklin Roosevelt's greatness will grow upon us all as distance gives us perspective. Like our very greatest Americans, in stature, he will become more and more heroic with the passing years.

I have known him, worked with him, and loved him for so many years, that I cannot say more now—except to express the sympathy we all feel for his brave wife and devoted children.

Mr. VANDENBERG. Mr. President, words are pathetic messengers. In this hour of anxious tragedy, when the bowed hearts of all the civilized earth join ours this fateful morning in humble, poignant sorrow that Franklin Delano Roosevelt, the thirty-second President of the United States, has been gathered to his fathers, nothing that we say here can add to the glory of his stature or to the measure of our grief. He belongs now to history, where he leaves a mark which not even rushing centuries can erase.

Those who were his loyal opposition, no less than those who were his intimate associates, have always recognized in him a rare crusader for his human faiths, an amazing genius in behalf of his always vigorous ideals, a valiant knight in the armor of his commandership as he waged global war. We join the Nation and the world upon their knees this sorrowing morning before his deeply honored bier.

He bravely mastered his own physical handicap with a courage which never lapsed as he fought his way to an unprecedented pinnacle at home and to dominant influence around the world. His untimely death will be mourned at every hearthstone, and on every battle front where freedom wins the victory to which he literally gave his life. A successful peace must be his monument.

Mr. President, a new President of the United States has stepped from the Senate Chamber to take over responsibility in this critical hour. America moves on, mourning her great dead and pledging her loyalty to a new leader who grasps the torch of our destiny and faces the future unafraid.

I am instructed by the minority conference of the Senate to report that it met this morning and dispatched the following message to the President of the United States:

In this critical and sorrowing hour, when you are called to the supreme responsibility of the Republic, we send you this expression of our faith and trust in you, and the assurance of our sustaining prayers. We shall cooperate with you for the winning of the war and a successful peace at home and abroad. We have directed a committee to call upon you at your convenience to advise with you.

Mr. President, when the country staggered 80 years ago under the awful impact of the news that Abraham Lincoln was dead, James A. Garfield concluded a messsage to the Nation with ringing words, which I now make my own, "God reigns, and the Government in Washington still lives."

Mr. CONNALLY. Mr. President, in the death of Franklin D. Roosevelt the world has lost its outstanding leader in the cause of peace, human progress, and welfare. He exerted a tremendous influence upon the world with regard to the establishment of an instrumentality for world peace and world security. I know that it would be his wish that this Nation and people continue to go forward in the cause which was close to his heart.

It is gratifying to know from the lips of the new President and from the lips of those who are directly concerned with the international affairs of the United States, that this work shall go on, and that at San Francisco we hope to realize the ambitions and the dreams of Franklin D. Roosevelt in the establishment of a world organization for peace and security.

Mr. President, while we are surrounded by the gloom of grief, while our people are bowed under the tremendous burdens that that grief brings us, I feel that Franklin Roosevelt died as he would have wished to die, in the midst of his duties and responsibilities and surrounded with the great tasks in which he wrought so wonderfully. I have always believed that if I were a farmer I should love to be called to my fathers out in my fields, surrounded by growing crops and lowing herds. If I worked in a shop, I should wish to be called amidst my tools and the implements of my toil. If I were an attorney at the bar, I should love to be called when I was pleading a cause which I regarded as just and right. If I were a statesman, I should love to feel that with my last expiring breath I had endeavored to advance the cause of human progress and development. If I were a soldier, I should prefer to die with a sword in my hand.

So I believe the President died as he would wish to die. He died with the armor upon him which he had worn so gallantly, and with a sword in his hand, fighting for triumph in this war and for the establishment of an instrumentality for peace.

I know that the new President—President Truman—will carry on the great work left in his hands. Already he has given expression to that purpose and that ambition—a purpose which will have the aid, support, and advice, not only of the Senate but of all responsible Government officials. I am confident that

President Truman will grasp the banner which has fallen from the lifeless hands of our great leader and will carry it on toward the achievement of our high purposes and our lofty ambitions.

The ACTING PRESIDENT pro tempore. The question is on agreeing to the resolution submitted by the Senator from Kentucky.

The resolution was unanimously agreed to.

The ACTING PRESIDENT pro tempore appointed the following Senators to attend the funeral services at the White House: Mr. McKellar, Mr. Barkley, Mr. White, Mr. George, Mr. Hayden, Mr. Wagner, Mr. Vandenberg, Mr. Connally, Mr. Thomas of Utah, Mr. Green, Mr. Mead, Mr. Tunnell, Mr. Millikin, Mr. Wherry, Mr. Cordon, and Mr. Saltonstall.

The ACTING PRESIDENT pro tempore also appointed the following Senators to attend the funeral at Hyde Park: Mr. Barkley, Mr. White, Mr. La Follette, Mr. Wagner, Mr. Austin, Mr. Hatch, Mr. O'Mahoney, Mr. Guffey, Mr. Pepper, Mr. Hill, Mr. Mead, Mr. Lucas, Mr. Burton, Mr. Maybank, Mr. Ball, Mr. Ferguson, and Mr. McMahon.

Mr. BARKLEY. Mr. President, as a further mark of respect to the memory of the late President of the United States, I move that the Senate adjourn until Monday next.

The motion was unanimously agreed; and (at 12 o'clock and 38 minutes p. m.) the Senate adjourned until Monday, April 16, 1945, at 12 o'clock meridian.

FRANKLIN DELANO ROOSEVELT

MONDAY, *April 16, 1945.*

The Senate met in executive session at 12 o'clock meridian.

The Chaplain, Rev. Frederick Brown Harris, D. D., offered the following prayer:

O God of birth and of death, God of the living and of the living dead, in whose hands are the souls of the righteous, in merciful pity Thou seest the startled, saddened faces of Thy children of every kindred and clime lifted to Thee in sobbing sorrow. We cry unto Thee from an earth which seems strangely poorer since it gently opened to receive the discarded mortal garment of Thy servant, Franklin Delano.

O Thou help of the helpless and of those who walk in the valley of the shadow of death, we give Thee thanks for the work and worth of this greatest captain of his time, when revolutions have shaken the earth and ancient social landmarks have been swept away with the flood and fury of human discontent. For his clear vision of the nature and purpose of satanic forces which threatened to engulf the world, for his fine scorn of the snobbery of class and color, for his heroic triumph over bodily affliction and disability—a precious gift to our shattered sons who return from battle to face the same test— for his steadfast faith in the processes of democracy as the hope of today and the wave of the future, for his brave rebuke to all who would drag Americanism to the level of differing backgrounds rather than to lift it to the dream of common goals, we praise Thee, Thou master of all good workmen.

Upon his dearest in the bowed circle of grief pour the consolation of Thy love and the assurance that he has but entered another and larger room in the Father's many-mansioned house.

Earnestly we pray for the anointing of Thy grace and the undergirding of Thy strength and the spirit of wisdom and understanding upon his successor in the high office, who steps from this Chamber and emerges from the loins of the common people to lead in the most awesome hour of history. Facing burdens and tasks too heavy for any man, use him as the channel of Thy purpose as in every crisis Thou hast used men of humble and contrite heart.

With him as the symbol of our national dedication and with our allies in this fight to make men free, we here highly resolve that the peace that is to be and the world united for peace and progress and an ampler life for all mankind shall be the high white monument leaping to the skies in memory of our lost leader. In the name of the blessed Lord whom he adored. Amen.

Mr. HATCH. Mr. President, the press of the Nation, the radio, through its programs and by its commentators, leaders in Congress, officials of the Nation, men and women in every walk of life—in fact, all the people of America—without regard to politics or other selfish consideration, have responded in our Nation's hour of sorrow, sadness, and tragedy in a manner such as the world has never before seen. Not as a public official but as an American citizen, I rise today to express my gratitude for the superbly wonderful way in which these tremendous forces have met what to a less courageous people might have meant disaster.

Press and radio—friend and foe of the previous administration alike—through editorial comment, through the news services and in every possible way, rose to the occasion with a patriotism never before witnessed in any country. Had the communications systems been directed and controlled, as they are in many countries of the world, the tributes to the departed Commander in Chief and the good will expressed for the incoming President could not have shown a more united spirit than was demonstrated here in free America by concerted, purely voluntary, and wholly cooperative effort inspired only by patriotic devotion to the Nation's welfare.

That same spirit of unswerving patriotism was manifest in every town and city throughout the land. In the pulpits of the churches, in memorial halls, in thronging crowds lining city streets and country lanes, America spoke her voice of sublime courage, faith, and confidence.

Let me now, Mr. President, in simple words, express to all of these and to every American, no matter where he lives or where he serves, on the battlefields or in civil life, my own great pride and faith in my country, her people, and her future, for, possessed by such indomitable courage, by such supreme faith, America will meet, overcome, and conquer every enemy of freedom and liberty on battlefield or domestic front. The spirit of a great people marches on—confident, triumphant, and unfraid—to the end, Mr. President, in the words of an immortal American, "that government of the people, by the people, and for the people shall not perish from the earth."

A message from the House of Representatives, by Mr. Swanson, one of its reading clerks, communicated to the Senate the resolutions of the House adopted as a tribute to the memory of Hon. Franklin Delano Roosevelt, late the President of the United States.

The PRESIDENT pro tempore laid before the Senate radiograms of condolences on the death of the late President Franklin Delano Roosevelt, which were ordered to lie on the table and to be printed in the Record, as follows:

FRANKLIN DELANO ROOSEVELT

MARACAIBO, *April 13, 1945.*

Congress of the United States of North America, Washington, D. C.:

In this hour of irreparable loss for the people of North America and the world, we unite our voice in expressing our condolence and great sympathy.

JEWISH COLONY OF MARACAIBO,
ELIAS ABADI, *President.*
JAIME GELMAN, *Secretary.*

———

MEXICO.

Congress of the United States, North American Capital, Washington, D. C.:

The National Anti-Nazi-Fascist Committee expresses its profound sorrow over the death of the great statesman and democrat, His Excellency Franklin D. Roosevelt. It constitutes an irreparable loss to all humanity and to the people of the United States.

For the National Committee:

The PRESIDENT,
ALFREDO FELIX DIAZ ESCOBAR.

FRIDAY, *May 24, 1946.*

A message from the House of Representatives, by Mr. Maurer, one of its reading clerks, announced that the House had agreed to a concurrent resolution (H. Con. Res. 152) providing for a joint session of Congress for the purpose of holding appropriate exercises in commemoration of the life, character, and public services of the late Franklin D. Roosevelt, former President of the United States, in which it requested the concurrence of the Senate.

SATURDAY, *June 1, 1946.*

The PRESIDING OFFICER (Mr. Huffman in the chair) laid before the Senate House Concurrent Resolution 152, which was read, as follows:

Resolved by the House of Representatives (the Senate concurring), That Monday, the 1st day of July 1946, be set aside as the day upon which there

(40)

shall be held a joint session of the Senate and the House of Representatives for appropriate exercises in commemoration of the life, character, and public service of the late Franklin D. Roosevelt, former President of the United States.

That a joint committee, to consist of three Senators and five Members of the House of Representatives, to be appointed by the President pro tempore of the Senate and the Speaker of the House of Representatives, respectively, shall be named, with full power to make all arrangements and publish a suitable program for the joint session of Congress herein authorized, and to issue the invitations hereinafter mentioned.

That invitations shall be extended to the President of the United States, the members of the Cabinet, the Chief Justice and Associate Justices of the Supreme Court of the United States, and such other invitations shall be issued as to the said committee shall seem best.

That all expenses incurred by the committee in the execution of the provisions of this resolution shall be paid, one-half from the contingent fund of the Senate and one-half from the contingent fund of the House of Representatives.

Mr. BARKLEY. I move that the Senate concur in the House concurrent resolution.

The motion was agreed to.

WEDNESDAY, *June 5, 1946.*

The PRESIDENT pro tempore. House Concurrent Resolution 152, providing for a joint session of the Congress on Monday, July 1, 1946, for the purpose of holding appropriate exercises in commemoration of the life, character, and public services of the late Franklin D. Roosevelt, President of the United States, has been duly adopted by both Houses. Under the terms of that resolution, the President of the Senate is directed to appoint a committee representing the Senate. On that committee the Chair appoints the Senator from Georgia [Mr. Russell], the Senator from Illinois [Mr. Lucas], and the Senator from California [Mr. Knowland].

Proceedings
in the
House of Representatives

Proceedings in the House of Representatives

✣

The House met at 12 o'clock noon.

Rt. Rev. Msgr. Patrick J. McCormick, rector, Catholic University of America, offered the following prayer:

Out of the depths have I cried unto Thee, O Lord. Lord, hear my voice: Let Thine ears be attentive to the voice of my supplication.

Almighty and merciful Father, who, in Thy inscrutable judgment and unsearchable way, hast called unto Thyself the soul of Franklin Delano Roosevelt, Thy faithful servant, whom Thou didst permit to lead and govern our people during a portentous period in our life as a nation, we bow in humble submission to Thy holy will. In this hour of national sadness and grief we turn to Thee, the God of all consolation and hope, and we plead for him, for with Thee there is merciful forgiveness and plenteous redemption, that he may have the reward of eternal happiness; we plead also for ourselves, our country, and Nation, that what has been gained and won for us by a life that was unselfishly spent to bring to all his fellows the means to live in security and prosperity will be furthered by our efforts and prospered by Thee. We pray for victory over our enemies, over those forces of evil that threatened and would have destroyed our achievements as a nation and our ideals for a better and fuller life; and we pray that in a common victory with our allies we may soon restore to the nations of the earth, to all mankind, the blessings of freedom and peace; this we beseech Thee through the merits of Thy Son, our Lord and Saviour, Jesus Christ. Amen.

FRANKLIN DELANO ROOSEVELT

A message from the Senate, by Mr. Gatling, its enrolling clerk, announced that the Senate had adopted the following resolution (S. Res. 119):

Resolved, That the Senate has learned with profound regret and sorrow of the death of the late President of the United States, Hon. Franklin Delano Roosevelt, illustrious statesman and leader in the Nation and in the world.

Resolved, That as a token of honor and in recognition of his eminent and distinguished public services to the Nation and to the world, the Presiding Officer of the Senate shall appoint a committee of 16 Senators to join a similar committee to be appointed on the part of the House of Representatives to attend the funeral services of the late President.

Resolved, That the Senate tenders its deep sympathy to the members of the family of the late President in their sad bereavement.

Resolved, That the Secretary communicate these resolutions to the House of Representatives and transmit a copy thereof to the family of the late President.

Resolved, That as a further mark of respect to the memory of the late President the Senate do now adjourn until Monday next.

The message also announced that pursuant to the above resolution, the Acting President pro tempore appointed Mr. McKellar, Mr. Barkley, Mr. White, Mr. George, Mr. Hayden, Mr. Wagner, Mr. Vandenberg, Mr. Connally, Mr. Thomas of Utah, Mr. Green, Mr. Mead, Mr. Tunnell, Mr. Millikin, Mr. Wherry, Mr. Cordon, and Mr. Saltonstall members of said committee on the part of the Senate.

Mr. McCormack. Mr. Speaker, I offer a resolution (H. Res. 216) and ask for its immediate consideration.

The Clerk read the resolution, as follows:

Resolved, That the House of Representatives has learned with profound regret and sorrow of the death of the late President of the United States, Hon. Franklin Delano Roosevelt, illustrious statesman and leader in the Nation and in the world.

Resolved, That as a token of honor and in recognition of his eminent and distinguished public services to the Nation and to the world the Speaker of the House shall appoint a committee of 15 Members of the House to join a similar committee appointed on the part of the Senate to attend the funeral services of the late President.

Resolved, That the House tenders its deep sympathy to the members of the family of the late President in their sad bereavement.

Resolved, That the Clerk communicate these resolutions to the Senate and transmit a copy thereof to the family of the late President.

The resolution was agreed to.

The SPEAKER. The Chair appoints the following Members of the House to attend the funeral services at the White House: Mr. Rayburn, Mr. Doughton of North Carolina, Mr. Vinson, Mr. Bland, Mr. Bloom, Mr. Cannon of Missouri, Mr. Cochran, Mr. Ramspeck, Mr. Snyder, Mr. Curley, Mr. Martin of Massachusetts, Mr. Woodruff of Michigan, Mrs. Rogers of Massachusetts, Mr. Jenkins, and Mr. Auchincloss; and the following Members of the House to attend the funeral at Hyde Park: Mr. Rayburn, Mr. McCormack, Mr. Sabath, Mr. Lea, Mrs. Norton, Mr. Cooper, Mr. Bulwinkle, Mr. May, Mr. Peterson of Florida, Mr. Quinn of New York, Mr. Martin of Massachusetts, Mr. Halleck, Mr. Arends, Mr. LeFevre, and Mr. Baldwin of New York.

The SPEAKER. The Clerk will report the remainder of the resolution.

The Clerk read as follows:

Resolved, That as a further mark of respect to the memory of the late President the House do now adjourn.

The resolution was agreed to; accordingly (at 12 o'clock and 5 minutes p. m.) the House adjourned until Monday, April 16, 1945, at 12 o'clock noon.

FRANKLIN DELANO ROOSEVELT

Thursday, *May 23, 1946.*

Mr. Bulwinkle. Mr. Speaker, I ask unanimous consent for the immediate consideration of House Concurrent Resolution 152.

The Clerk read as follows:

Resolved, That Monday, the 1st day of July 1946, be set aside as the day upon which there shall be held a joint session of the Senate and the House of Representatives for appropriate exercises in commemoration of the life, character, and public service of the late Franklin D. Roosevelt, former President of the United States.

That a joint committee, to consist of three Senators and five Members of the House of Representatives, to be appointed by the President pro tempore of the Senate and the Speaker of the House of Representatives, respectively, shall be named, with full power to make all arrangements and publish a suitable program for the joint session of Congress herein authorized, and to issue the invitations hereinafter mentioned.

That invitations shall be extended to the President of the United States, the members of the Cabinet, the Chief Justice and Associate Justices of the Supreme Court of the United States, and such other invitations shall be issued as to the said committee shall seem best.

That all expenses incurred by the committee in the execution of the provisions of this resolution shall be paid, one-half from the contingent fund of the Senate and one-half from the contingent fund of the House of Representatives.

The Speaker. Is there objection to the request of the gentleman from North Carolina?

There was no objection.

The resolution was agreed to.

A motion to reconsider was laid on the table.

FRANKLIN DELANO ROOSEVELT

MONDAY, *June 3, 1946.*

A message from the Senate, by Mr. Frazier, its legislative clerk, announced that the Senate had passed without amendment a concurrent resolution of the House of the following title:

H. Con. Res. 152. Concurrent resolution providing for a joint session of Congress for the purpose of holding appropriate exercises in commemoration of the life, character, and public services of the late Franklin D. Roosevelt, former President of the United States.

WEDNESDAY, *June 5, 1946.*

The SPEAKER. Pursuant to the provisions of House Concurrent Resolution 152, Seventy-ninth Congress, the Chair appoints as members of the joint committee to make arrangements for the joint session to be held on Monday, July 1, 1946, for appropriate exercises in commemoration of the life, character, and public service of the late Franklin D. Roosevelt, the following Members on the part of the House: Mr. Bulwinkle, Mr. Walter, Mrs. Douglas of Illinois, Mrs. Rogers of Massachusetts, and Mr. LeFevre.

Tributes

Tributes

*

AFGHANISTAN

LEGATION ROYALE D'AFGHANISTAN,
Washington, D. C., April 12, 1945.

His Excellency Mr. EDWARD R. STETTINIUS, Jr.,
Secretary of State,
Washington, D. C.

EXCELLENCY: It is with profound grief and the deepest sorrow that I hear of the untimely death of the beloved President of the United States of America, Franklin Delano Roosevelt.

The United States and indeed the whole peace-loving world has lost a leader and a friend whose greatness and courage will never be forgotten. It can only be hoped that his ideal of a world of free peoples, toward which he strived in life and for which he died, will be brought soon to a reality.

Please accept my most heartfelt sympathy and that of my country for you, Excellency, and your government, the family of Mr. Roosevelt, and the citizens of The United States of America who mourn their overwhelming loss.

Most sincerely yours,

A. HOSAYN AZIZ.

ALBANIA

TIRANA, *April 13, 1945.*

His Excellency Mr. HARRY TRUMAN,
President of the United States of America,
Washington:

It is with the most profound grief that I learned of the mourning of the Republic of the United States in the irreparable loss which it has suffered in the person of its illustrious President His Excellency Franklin Roosevelt. I hasten to express to Your Excellency in my name and in the name of the Democratic Government of Albania with which the entire Albanian people are associated the expressing of most moving condolences and I beg you to convey this to the Government of the Republic and the noble American nation.

(s) ENVER HOXHA,
President of the Council of Ministers of the
Democratic Government of Albania.

(53)

FRANKLIN DELANO ROOSEVELT

ARGENTINA

BUENOS AIRES, *April 13, 1945.*

His Excellency HARRY S. TRUMAN,
President of the United States of America,
Washington.

The passing of the great and illustrious President Franklin D. Roosevelt at a time when he was reaching the culmination of a magnificent work of which he was the principal artisan saddens all peoples of America equally. The loss of such a great statesman, a prominent figure of our times who fought so resolutely to guarantee the union of the Americas to consolidate the peace and the rule of right among nations, constitutes an irreparable loss for the world. President Roosevelt enters history as a symbol of faith in the essential freedoms of men. May the sentiments of fraternal sympathy of the Argentine people and Government reach the people and Government of the United States.

EDELMIRO J. FARRELL,
President of the Argentine Nation.

AUSTRALIA

APRIL 13, 1945.

Message from the Right Honourable JOHN CURTIN, Prime Minister of the Commonwealth of Australia

We have been profoundly shocked at news of tragic death of your President. For many years his words and his work have been an inspiration to all who have at heart welfare of human race. With infinite skill and patience he worked to preserve the peace of world and when all hope of peace was gone and war began he threw himself into struggle for survival of democracy with unremitting self-sacrifice and with a courage which has brought victory within our reach.

Name of Mr. Roosevelt is a household word in this country and our admiration of his personal qualities no less than of his work as leader of your great people was unlimited. All Australians today feel a personal sorrow at loss of a true friend, an inspiring world leader and a great humanitarian. His memory will be revered in Australia for all time.

FRANKLIN DELANO ROOSEVELT

BELGIUM

BRUSSELS, *April 13, 1945.*

Mr. HARRY S. TRUMAN,
  President of the United States of America,
             Washington, D. C.

President Roosevelt died at the moment victory was going to crown his efforts. One of the world's greatest champions of liberty, one of the most strongly convinced defenders of the existence of small nations died during his labors. His loss is an irreparable misfortune not only for the United States but for all the United Nations. The work of President Roosevelt remains as a guide for us. It symbolizes the ideal of understanding and peace among men of good will. I extend to Your Excellency Belgium's most profound condolences and mine.

CHARLES.

※

BOLIVIA

LA PAZ, *April 13, 1945.*

His Excellency HARRY S. TRUMAN,
  President of the United States of America,
             The White House:

I have the honor to express to Your Excellency the deep sense of sorrow of the Bolivian Government and people on the passing away of the illustrious President Franklin Delano Roosevelt, whom the American nations mourn 〔and〕 whose name is forever linked with them by his developing the Good Neighbor Policy, solidly binding the ties of friendship with the great Northern Republic, and firmly laying the bases of continental solidarity and friendly understanding between our peoples.

GUALBERTO VILLARROEL,
              President of Bolivia.

FRANKLIN DELANO ROOSEVELT

BRAZIL

RIO DE JANEIRO, *April 13, 1945.*

His Excellency HARRY S. TRUMAN,
President of the United States of America,
Washington, D. C.:

In my name, in that of the Government and of the Brazilians I express to Your Excellency, to the Government and people of the United States of America our most sincere condolences for the immense loss which the Americas and all free nations have just suffered in the death of President Franklin Delano Roosevelt. This news was received with the greatest consternation in Brazil, where the great statesman was the object of devoted friendship and unbounded admiration for his action as champion of the democracies and defender of oppressed peoples. The Brazilians will never forget the devotion and constant esteem which President Roosevelt manifested toward them.

GETULIO VARGAS,
President of the Republic of the United States of Brazil.

BULGARIA

SOFIA, *April 14, 1945.*

EDGAR STETINIUS,
Secretary of State for Foreign Affairs,
Washington.

The Bulgarian Government has entrusted me to beg you to convey to the President of the United States and to the American people the heartfelt condolences of the Ministerial Council and of my countrymen for the loss of the President Roosevelt. The news that this noble champion of freedom and democracy has passed into eternity has touched us deeply and has plunged Bulgarians of all walks of life in deep sorrow as we have all followed with greatest enthusiasm his untiring efforts to preserve the foundations of peace in the world and to guarantee the rights and liberties of small nations at the coming settlement of world peace.

PETCO STAYNOFF,
Bulgarian Minister for Foreign Affairs.

FRANKLIN DELANO ROOSEVELT

CANADA

OTTAWA, *April 13, 1945.*

His Excellency, The Hon. RAY ATHERTON,
    Ambassador of the United States of America,
                                    Ottawa.

Dear Mr. ATHERTON: The Prime Minister would be grateful if you would be good enough to convey the following message from the Prime Minister to the Honorable Edward R. Stettinius, Jr., Secretary of State:

"Personally and in my capacity as Secretary of State for External Affairs, I desire to send you the expression of my deepest sympathy in the personal loss which you have sustained in the death of President Roosevelt and in the added burden or responsibility which you have so suddenly been called upon to bear. You will need no assurance of my earnest desire to cooperate in fullest measure with you and of a like desire on the part of the Canadian government to cooperate with the government of the United States in seeking to meet the problems which confront the world of today, and which are of such vital concern to our two countries.

"W. L. MACKENZIE KING."

Yours sincerely,

C. A. ROBERTSON,
Under-Secretary of State for External Affairs.

CHILE

April 13, 1945.

His Excellency EDWARD R. STETTINIUS, JR.,
    The Secretary of State, Washington, D. C.

EXCELLENCY: With profound feeling I have received the kind communication of this date, by which Your Excellency officially informs me of the death of Franklin Delano Roosevelt, President of the United States of America, at Warm Springs, Georgia, at three thirty-five p. m. on April 12, 1945.

The Government of Chile, upon being appraised of this irreparable loss, instructed me to offer its sincerest condolences to the Government of the United States of America.

President Franklin Delano Roosevelt was the object of special devotion for the people of Chile, not only because of the high position he held, but also, and in exceptional manner, for his extraordinary personal capacity, for his exceptional courage, his firmness and clear vision, in the service and defense of liberty, democracy and other fundamental principles of civilization.

The propounding of the Good Neighbor Policy and the great benefits conferred by it on all the nations of the Hemisphere, contributes to make even more profound the emotion which in these sad circumstances is experienced by the people and Government of Chile, who have always looked upon the illustrious deceased as the leader of a cause of transcendental proportions in the destiny of the Continent.

The President of the Republic of Chile, Juan Antonio Ríos, wishes to associate himself in particular with the expression of the sorrow of his Government, and notwithstanding the direct communication made by him, he has requested me to reiterate his expression to Your Excellency.

In the communication to which I have the honor to respond, Your Excellency informs me that in conformity with the provisions of the Constitution, the office of President of the United States of America has devolved upon Harry S. Truman.

The Government of Chile desires to convey its sincerest wishes for the success of the new Administration.

I transmit these expressions to Your Excellency, and through your high intermediacy to the Government of the United States of America, with the profound emotion I personally feel at the decease of the illustrious President Franklin Delano Roosevelt, whose loss, notwithstanding the tremendous significance it assumes under present circumstances, has contributed to emphasize the civic values of this nation, in the exemplary observance of the democratic process.

Accept, Excellency, the renewed assurances of my highest consideration.

MARCIAL MORA.

CHINA

CHINESE EMBASSY,
Washington, April 17, 1945.

Honorable EDWARD R. STETTINIUS, JR.,
Secretary of State, Washington, D. C.

SIR: It is with deepest sorrow to acknowledge the receipt of your note of April 13, 1945, informing me of the death of Franklin Delano Roosevelt, President of the United States of America, which occurred at Warm Springs, Georgia, at three thirty-five p. m. on April 12, 1945.

FRANKLIN DELANO ROOSEVELT

I have duly reported to my Government of the sad tidings and of your announcement that in obedience to the prescriptions of the Constitution, the office of President has developed upon Harry S. Truman.

Accept, Sir, the renewed assurances of my highest consideration.

WEI TAO-MING.

COLOMBIA

BOGOTÁ, *April 13, 1945.*

His Excellency HARRY S. TRUMAN,
    President of the United States of America,
           Washington, D. C.:

In name of my people deeply moved by the death of President Roosevelt. I wish to express to Your Excellency the feeling of grief of Colombians. President Roosevelt had risen to the stature of the greatest men of America, to that of Washington, Bolivar, and San Martin, Jefferson and Lincoln. He was the interpreter of the conscience of the free world and without him the victory, the culmination of which we await very shortly, would have been, if not impossible, extraordinarily difficult. For our nations President Roosevelt was the creator and the defender of a policy which received in Mexico a few weeks ago its historical consecration as the American policy. And he was also the disseminator of principles of international conscience which are today those of the three Americas. And, with the aid of this continent they shall be, in a not distant day, the principles of the universe, if we wish just peace and true security. Roosevelt was our best neighbor and his country during the years of his term of office only increased in popularity, friendship, prestige among the nations of the hemisphere. There will not be, Excellency, a single place on earth where this news will not cause disturbance and regret because there was not a single one which under his stimulus and direction the efforts of the American people to free the world from fear, want, injustice, despotism did not reach. At this hour which is one of mourning for Colombia also we pray to God that the great nation over which you are going to preside will vigorously terminate the undertaking which Roosevelt began and that it will take courage in the thought that the virtues of the great American of our time, his generous and human spirit, resistance and adversity, intuition of the future, are those of your nation. Accept, Excellency, the manifestation of our solidarity with the grief of the United States.

ALFONSO LOPEZ,
President of Colombia.

FRANKLIN DELANO ROOSEVELT

COSTA RICA

SAN JOSE, *April 12, 1945.*

Mr. HARRY TRUMAN:

Deeply grieved by the distressing news of the death of Mr. Roosevelt extend through you to the North American Government and people the most regretful expression of condolence of the Government and people of Costa Rica which join you in this hour of grief. Repeat assurances of my consideration and remain your humble servant.

TEODORO PICADO,
President of Costa Rica.

CUBA

HABANA, *April 13, 1945.*

His Excellency HARRY S. TRUMAN,
President of the United States of America,
Washington, D. C.:

Profoundly affected by the regrettable death of His Excellency Franklin D. Roosevelt, President of your great friendly Nation, whose high qualities and personal attraction won my admiration and friendship and that of all Cubans, I hasten to express to Your Excellency the deep grief of the Government of Cuba and my personal grief for your misfortune. The death of so illustrious a statesman constitutes an immense and grievous loss for humanity and the cause of the United Nations.

RAMON GRAU SAN MARTÍN,
President of the Republic of Cuba.

CZECHOSLOVAKIA

The PRESIDENT OF THE UNITED STATES OF AMERICA,
Mr. HARRY S. TRUMAN,
Washington, D. C.:

Shortly after the Czechoslovak people have heard with emotion the message which President Roosevelt has sent me at the moment of the Czechoslovak Government's return to the liberated territory the report has reached me of his sudden death. I bow deeply to the great dead. In Mr. Roosevelt's death not only the United States but all the Allies have suffered an irreparable loss and the whole Czechoslovak people is profoundly grieved at this great blow. The tremendous work done by President Roosevelt for the liberation of the subjugated nations, his moral influence on the drafting of the principles of peace, freedom, and democracy for future generations will forever remain as historical contribution of his outstanding personality and thus also of his great country the United States of America to the well-being of the whole of mankind. Please accept Mr. President the expression of the profound grief of the whole Czechoslovak people at the death of the great President of the United States of America, F. D. Roosevelt.

DR. EDVARD BENEŠ.

DENMARK

ROYAL DANISH LEGATION,
Washington, D. C., April 14, 1945.

The Honorable EDWARD R. STETTINIUS, JR.,
   Secretary of State,
      Department of State, Washington, D. C.

SIR: I have the honor to acknowledge the receipt of your note of April 13th announcing to me the death of Franklin Delano Roosevelt, President of the United States of America.

I beg to convey to you, Mr. Secretary of State, my deep sympathy in the great loss thus sustained by the United States as well as by all freedom-loving nations.

My countrymen at home and all over the world are sharing the grief of the American people. In President Roosevelt they lost a true friend whose memory shall live forever in Denmark.

Accept, Sir, the renewed assurances of my highest consideration.

HENRIK KAUFFMANN.

DOMINICAN REPUBLIC

CIUDAD TRUJILLO, April 12, 1945.

Her Excellency Mrs. ELEANOR ROOSEVELT,
   Washington, D. C.:

Deeply shocked and touched, I hasten to send to you with the homage of my respect the expression of my most profound condolence on the occasion of the

FRANKLIN DELANO ROOSEVELT

decease of your illustrious husband, whereby the United States loses its most brilliant statesman and America and the world, the hero of peace and of justice.

RAFAEL L. TRUJILLO MOLINA,
President, Dominican Republic.

✿

ECUADOR

QUITO, *April 13, 1945.*

His Excellency HARRY TRUMAN,
Vice President of the United States,
White House, Washington:

I convey to Your Excellency in the name of the Ecuadoran people wholeheartedly for freedom, the rights of man and the moral concept of life the most profound grief at the sudden and unfortunate death of the illustrious President Roosevelt. The memory of this eminent magistrate who with Washington, Lincoln, Wilson will figure among the greatest men of the United States [and] will always be respected by the Latin-American people and by the citizens of the world who believe in ascending, spiritual and divine purpose of history, when in a fleeting instant and abusing the disorientation of a grieved world desirous of new horizons the mechanical defiant and violent arrogance of materialist totalitarianism was artificially accentuated. The voice of the illustrious President Roosevelt was raised clearly, sincerely, and bravely without vague generalities to condemn in a decisive way the person and acts of totalitarian tyrants. There was a time when Roosevelt was the only precise moral orientation of the peoples and when the economic interests claimed the dignity and sovereignty of Latin American nations must be suppressed the world of Franklin Delano Roosevelt proclaimed the Good Neighbor Policy that one respects himself by respecting equality among all states, the personality of nations and the norms of solidarity and cooperation. President Roosevelt falls as a hero of morality and of the spirit crushed in the extraordinary struggle in order that humanity and justice and democracy may be effective for humanity. The spirit of Roosevelt will be the prompt and definitive victory of freemen.

J. M. VELASCO IBARRA,
President of Ecuador.

(62)

FRANKLIN DELANO ROOSEVELT

EGYPT

CAIRO, *April 13, 1945.*

His Excellency HARRY TRUMAN,
Vice President of the United States of America,
The White House, Washington, D. C.:

I am deeply afflicted by the cruel loss which the United States has just suffered in the person of President Roosevelt whose name will be recorded in history as one of the most illustrious champions of democracy and human liberty. In rendering moved and admiring homage to the memory of the great leader who has passed on the eve of the final victory to which his indomitable energy and wise guidance of the American people have so powerfully contributed all Egypt and I, myself, wish to assure Your Excellency and the noble American Nation of our very sincere participation in their sorrow.

FAROUK R.

EL SALVADOR

EMBASSY OF EL SALVADOR,
Washington, April 14, 1945.

His Excellency EDWARD R. STETTINIUS, JR,
Secretary of State, Washington, D. C.

Mr. SECRETARY: I have received Your Excellency's kind note, dated April 13, in which you communicated to me the sad news of the death of His Excellency, Franklin Delano Roosevelt, President of the United States of America, which took place in Warm Springs, at 3:30 in the afternoon of April 12.

Your Excellency requests in that note that I transmit this sad news to my Government, and that I announce further that, in compliance with the provisions of the Constitution, the duties of the President have been assumed by His Excellency, Harry S. Truman, Vice President of the Republic.

In a separate note, I have expressed to Your Excellency the sincere association of the people and the Government of El Salvador in the mourning of the people and the Government of the United States of America. At the same time, I have had the opportunity to communicate to my Government, the information which Your Excellency transmitted to me in the note to which I have referred.

In reply to Your Excellency's courteous note, my Government has sent me the two radiograms, the text of which I copy hereinbelow:

"April 13. Ambassador Hector David Castro, Washington, D. C. I reply your radiogram yesterday referring death Excellency President Roosevelt.

News has caused sadness to Salvadoran people and Government and as tribute memory distinguished statesman and demonstration sympathy toward
United States of America, National Legislative Assembly decreed three days'
national mourning. Ask you reiterate our Government's condolence to that
friendly Government.

"A. ARGUELLO LOUCEL,
"Minister of Foreign Affairs."

"April 13. Ambassador Hector David Castro, Washington, D. C. I ask
you extend condolence to American Government stating to it that our Government designates you its special ambassador for funeral Excellency President
Roosevelt.

"ARTURO ARGUELLO LOUCEL,
"Minister of Foreign Affairs."

In communicating to Your Excellency the text of the radiograms which I
have just quoted, I have the honor and the deep regret of reiterating to Your
Excellency the sentiments of sorrow with which my Government has received
the unfortunate news of the loss of the illustrious Chief Executive of the
Federal Union.

I beg to ask that Your Excellency kindly extend my Government's sympathy
and my own to President Roosevelt's widow and distinguished family.

In my capacity as Special Ambassador of my Government, I shall attend this
afternoon the funeral services which will be held in the White House.

Accept, Excellency, the renewed assurances of my highest consideration.

HÉCTOR DAVID CASTRO,
Ambassador Designate of El Salvador.

ETHIOPIA

EDWARD R. STETTINIUS,
Secretary of State, Washington, D. C.:

With the American Nation and the entire World Ethiopa is plunged into
profoundest grief at the death of President Roosevelt. In his passing the
World has suffered a cruel and irreparable loss at a time when his leadership
was indispensable for guiding the World back to the paths of Peace. Kindly
convey to the family of the President and to the American Nation my deepest
sympathy.

BITWODDED MAKONNEN ENDALKACHAU,
Prime Minister of Ethiopia.

FRANKLIN DELANO ROOSEVELT

FINLAND

HELSINKI, *April 13, 1945.*

Mrs. ROOSEVELT,
  Washington:

I have the honour to express my sincerest sympathy in your bereavement and in the loss the people of America have sustained. I assure you of the high esteem in which the Finnish people will keep the memory of the great American statesman and his championship of the rights of the nations. The name of President Franklin Roosevelt will not be forgotten in far distant Finland.

MANNERHEIM,
President of the Republic of Finland.

❧

GREAT BRITAIN

BRITISH EMBASSY,
Washington, D. C., April 16, 1945.

The Honourable EDWARD R. STETTINIUS, JR.,
  Secretary of State of the United States,
      Washington, D. C.

EXCELLENCY: It is with the deepest regret that I have received your note of April 13th announcing to me that the death of Franklin Delano Roosevelt, President of the United States of America, occurred at Warm Springs, Georgia, at three thirty-five p. m. on April 12th, 1945. I have not failed to communicate this grievous news to my Government and to inform them that in obedience to the prescriptions of the Constitution, the office of President has devolved upon Harry S. Truman.

I now have the honour, on behalf of His Majesty's Government in the United Kingdom, to express to you, Mr. Secretary, profound sympathy with the Government and people of the United States in the incalculable loss which they have suffered through the death of a great President. I beg leave to add an expression of my own condolence and sympathy, with which all the members of the staffs of the British Embassy, the British Consulates and the British Missions and other organisations in the United States desire to be associated.

Accept, Excellency, the renewed assurance of my highest consideration.

HALIFAX.

FRANKLIN DELANO ROOSEVELT

FRANCE

PARIS, *April 13, 1945.*

President TRUMAN,
    Washington:

It is with great emotion and profound sadness that the French Government and people learn of the death of the great President Roosevelt. He was, in the eyes of all humanity, the symbolic champion of the great cause for which the United Nations have so suffered and fought in the cause of liberty. He was not able to live long enough to see the triumphant end of this war in which his noble country is struggling in the front rank. At least, the decisive successes to which he has so powerfully contributed gave him the certainty of victory before he succumbed at his post of combat. He leaves the world an imperishable example and an essential message. That message will be heard. He was from his first day to his last a faithful friend of France. France admired him and loved him. I express to you, Mr. President, its fervent homage to the memory of President Franklin Delano Roosevelt and its sentiments of extreme sympathy and of grieving friendship for the great American people.

GENERAL DE GAULLE.

GREECE

The PRESIDENT OF THE UNITED STATES,
    White House, Washington, D. C.:

The untimely death of Franklin Roosevelt deprives mankind of an inspired architect of victory and a tireless champion of peace. To me personally and to Greece his death means the loss of a sincere and beloved friend whom I am sure we will find again in your person. I send to the American people the expression of my profound sorrow on the passing of their great leader and I pray, Mr. President, that under your inspired leadership they may soon see the realization of all their hopes and aspirations.

GEORGE II R.

FRANKLIN DELANO ROOSEVELT

GUATEMALA

GUATEMALA CITY, April 12, 1945.

His Excellency HARRY TRUMAN,
  Vice President of the United States of America,
    White House, Washington, D. C.:

In the name of the people and Government of Guatemala and in my own I hasten to express to Your Excellency the sentiments of heartfelt sympathy on the decease of His Excellency Franklin Delano Roosevelt, President of your great and friendly nation. The world loses the greatest of its contemporary statesmen and democracy one of its staunchest defenders. I renew to Your Excellency the assurances of my highest and most distinguished consideration.

JUAN JOSÉ ARÉVALO,
President of Guatemala.

❧

HAITI

PORT-AU-PRINCE, April 12, 1945.

Mrs. ROOSEVELT,
  White House, Washington, D. C.:

It is with the most profound grief that I have just learned of the death of President Roosevelt. Your grief is profound. Please believe me, dear Madame, when I say that I share it with you in mourning for that great personal and proven friend of the Haitian people. I beg you to accept the assurance of my respectful sympathy on this sad occasion and that of Madame Lescot who joins me in conveying to you our heartfelt condolences.

LESCOT,
President of Haiti.

❧

HONDURAS

TEGUCIGALPA, April 12, 1945.

Mrs. ELEANOR ROOSEVELT,
  White House, Washington, D. C.:

I beg you to accept, in the name of the Honduran people, the Government over which I preside, and in my own, the expression of our most sincere and heartfelt condolences on the decease of that great statesman and great friend of America, Franklin D. Roosevelt. Please accept the expressions of sympathy of the Honduran nation.

TIBURCIO CARÍAS A.

FRANKLIN DELANO ROOSEVELT

ICELAND

His Excellency HARRY S. TRUMAN,
President of the United States of America, Washington:

I and the people of Iceland have learned with great regret the news of the death of President Roosevelt. Please accept for yourself, your Government, and the people of the United States the condolences of myself and the people of Iceland upon this loss to your people which is at the same time the greatest loss to the whole democratic world, including Iceland. The Icelandic people will always uphold the memory of this great statesman with gratefulness and devotion.

SVEINN BJORNSSON,
President of Iceland.

IRAN

His Excellency Mr. STETTINIUS,
Secretary of State, Washington, D. C.:

I am profoundly shocked to hear the sad news of the death of Mr. Roosevelt, late President of the United States of America. Please accept my sincere condolences and kindly convey same to Mrs. Roosevelt and to all members of the deceased's family.

HOMAYOUNDJAH,
Acting Foreign Minister.

IRAQ

The PRESIDENT OF THE UNITED STATES OF AMERICA,
Washington, D. C.:

I am deeply grieved to hear the tragic news of the death of President Roosevelt. In the name of His Majesty King Faisal II and on my own behalf and that of the people of Iraq I offer to you and to the American people our sincerest sympathy in the death of your beloved President.

ABDUL ILAH,
Regent of Iraq.

FRANKLIN DELANO ROOSEVELT

IRELAND

President TRUMAN,
Washington, D. C.:

I have learned with profound regret of the death of President Roosevelt and I offer you my deepest sympathy in the sorrow which has befallen you and the whole American people.

DOUGLAS HYDE,
President of Ireland.

ITALY

WASHINGTON, D. C., April 16, 1945.

Mrs. ELEANOR ROOSEVELT,
The White House, Washington, D. C.

MY DEAR MRS. ROOSEVELT: On behalf of the Lieutenant General of the Kingdom of Italy, H. R. H. Prince Umberto di Savoia, I have the honor to convey to you His expressions of profound sorrow and heartfelt sympathy for the passing of President Roosevelt.

His death is not only a reason of grief to you and to the American nation, but to all mankind who has lost in him a stanch defender of right and justice for peoples as well as nations.

The Italian people, who have received from him in their hour of national distress so many proofs of generosity, aid, and comprehension, will miss him greatly and will always hold the most reverent and grateful memories of him.

Please accept, my dear Mrs. Roosevelt, the renewed expression of H. R. H. the Prince of Piedmont's condolences together with my deepest sympathy.

Respectfully yours,

ALBERTO TARCHIANI,
Italian Ambassador.

LATVIA

LATVIAN LEGATION,
Washington, D. C., April 13, 1945.

The Honorable EDWARD R. STETTINIUS, Jr.,
Secretary of State, Washington.

SIR: On behalf of the Latvian nation and of myself I beg you to accept my condolences and expressions of deepest sympathy in connection with the unexpected death of President Roosevelt.

FRANKLIN DELANO ROOSEVELT

The late President was always a great and staunch friend of the small nations, and his just and benevolent views expressed in the Atlantic Charter will remain as a beacon of hope and light for oppressed peoples. The Latvian nation will cherish forever the memory of Franklin Delano Roosevelt as a sincere friend and champion of their cause.

Accept, Sir, the renewed assurances of my highest consideration.

Dr. ALFRED BILMANIS,
Latvian Minister.

LEBANON

BEYROUTH, *April 13, 1945.*

His Excellency HARRY S. TRUMAN,
President of the United States of America,
Washington, D. C.:

I have been profoundly affected by the death of the illustrious statesman His Excellency President Roosevelt the perfect incarnation of the principles of international justice and solidarity. I share the universally felt grief on seeing his great figure pass on the eve of the day on which his valued cooperation in the future tasks of the peace was impatiently awaited by the United Nations. I beg Your Excellency and the American people to accept the expressions of sympathy which I send them in the name of my compatriots and in my own name. Lebanon will always preserve faithfully the memory of this generous man whose active friendship has never failed it.

BECHARA KHALIL EL KHOURY.

LIECHTENSTEIN

VADUZ.

His Excellency the PRESIDENT OF THE UNITED STATES,
White House, Washington, D. C.:

With deepest regret I heard the sad news of the sudden death of President Roosevelt. I beg Your Excellency to accept my most sincere sympathies also from the Government and the people of Liechtenstein.

FRANZ JOSEPH,
Prince Liechtenstein.

FRANKLIN DELANO ROOSEVELT

LITHUANIA

LITHUANIAN LEGATION,
Washington, D. C., April 13, 1945.

The Honorable EDWARD R. STETTINIUS, Jr.,
    Secretary of State,
        Department of State, Washington, D. C.

SIR: Permit me to express to the Government of the United States my sincere sympathy in the great loss caused by the death of The Honorable Franklin Delano Roosevelt, President of the United States.

I have the honor to request you to be good enough to convey to Mrs. Roosevelt my deepest sympathy in her bereavement.

Accept, Sir, the renewed assurances of my highest consideration.

P. ŽADEIKIS,
Minister of Lithuania.

LUXEMBOURG

LONDON.

The PRESIDENT OF THE UNITED STATES,
    White House, Washington:

On the occasion of the death of President Roosevelt at the climax of his long and arduous labour in the service of his country and of mankind I convey to you the expression of my most profound condolence. The President was a great and faithful friend to me and to my country throughout the war. We owe him a debt which can never be repaid and it is with peculiar emotion that we share in the sorrow of the American people deprived in the hour of victory of their great leader in the struggle for human rights and liberties.

CHARLOTTE,
Grandduchess of Luxembourg.

FRANKLIN DELANO ROOSEVELT

MEXICO

MEXICO, *April 12, 1945.*

His Excellency HARRY TRUMAN,
President of the United States of America,
Washington, D. C.:

Deeply distressed by the passing of illustrious President of the United States, His Excellency Franklin D. Roosevelt, offer Your Excellency the condolences of the Mexican Government and people, together with my own most regretful ones for the irreparable loss of the one who being the first citizen of the United States, at the same time stood out as the most prominent figure of present times. Mexico and the other Latin American nations are indebted to him particularly for the renowned good-neighbor policy which marks the point of departure of a new era in Inter-American relations. Beg Your Excellency to accept on so sad an occasion the assurances of my highest and most distinguished consideration.

MANUEL AVILA CAMACHO,
President of the United Mexican States.

MONACO

MONACO, *April 13, 1945.*

His Excellency the PRESIDENT OF THE UNITED STATES OF AMERICA,
Washington, D. C.:

I am profoundly grieved, Mr. President, by the sorrow which afflicts the United States. The death of the great and noble figure of President Franklin Roosevelt is a misfortune for entire humanity and the Principality is sadly afflicted. I beg Your Excellency to accept my warmest sympathy.

LOUIS,
Prince of Monaco.

MOROCCO

EMBASSY OF FRANCE IN THE UNITED STATES,
Washington, April 27, 1945.

The DEPARTMENT OF STATE,
Washington, D. C.:

The Embassy of France in the United States presents its compliments to the Department of State and has the honor to transmit to it, below, the text of a

message from His Majesty the Sultan of Morocco, Sidi Mohammed ben Yous-
sef, on the occasion of the death of Mr. Roosevelt.

"Having received the news of the grievous loss which the United States of
America has just suffered, we address to you, in our name and in the name of all
of our subjects, the expression of our deepest sympathy and we request you to
convey to Mrs. Roosevelt and to her family the expression of our sorrow because of the loss of the great man whose great heartedness and inestimable
qualities we had the honor to appreciate on the occasion of his stay in
Morocco."

The Embassy avails itself [etc.].

❧

NETHERLANDS

LONDON.

The PRESIDENT,
 Washington, D. C.:

I should like to offer the American people my deep sympathy in their great
loss which my people and I fully share. He gave his life for our common cause
and the Netherlands will ever cherish his name.

WILHELMINA R.

❧

NEW ZEALAND

NEW ZEALAND LEGATION,
Washington, D. C., April 13, 1945.

Hon. E. R. STETTINIUS, Jr.,
 Secretary of State, Washington, D. C.

DEAR MR. SECRETARY: I have been directed by the Hon. Walter Nash,
Acting Prime Minister of New Zealand, to convey to you the following
message from the Government of New Zealand:

"We have learned with the deepest regret the tragic news of the death of
President Roosevelt. His passing is a blow to the free peoples of all the countries of the world. Democracy had no greater friend, and his inspiring leadership in its cause will ever be remembered. He was the ardent champion of the
underprivileged, not only in his own country but everywhere. His contribution towards lifting the world out of the depression was unsurpassed. His

wise measures and kindly counsel were listened to and were to the benefit of all the people of all countries. We here in New Zealand will ever cherish a grateful memory of his friendship and inspiration both before and during the present world war. His guidance of his country during the prewar period and the early years of the war came second only to his unparalleled contribution after the United States entered the conflict. Lend-Lease among other epoch-making conceptions will keep his memory green in all countries that have been saved by its help. His decisions as Commander in Chief of the United States Forces have made a major contribution in the direction of the conflict towards the victory we hope soon to enjoy. Like earlier great leaders he has led the world towards the victory that will make possible peace among the Nations, but he will not be here to enjoy the fruits of the work which he has done. He was a citizen of the world in the greatest and truest sense and his death is an irreparable loss to the cause of freedom.

"To Mrs. Roosevelt and her family, to his colleagues in the Government, and to all United States citizens, the Government and people of New Zealand and its Island territories extend their sympathy at the loss of a great son of a great people."

Yours sincerely,

JOHN S. REID, *Chargé d'Affaires.*

NICARAGUA

GENERAL SOMOSA'S CAMP,
San Gabriel, April 13, 1945.

His Excellency Mr. HARRY TRUMAN,
Washington, D. C.:

In the name of the Government of the people of Nicaragua and myself I convey to Your Excellency and the great North American people the deepest sorrow at the death of the illustrious Franklin D. Roosevelt to the bereavement of all the free men of the world. At the same time I salute Your Excellency as the new great leader of the North American people in the tremendous struggle for human liberty.

A. SOMOSA,
President of Nicaragua.

FRANKLIN DELANO ROOSEVELT

NORWAY

LONDON.

President TRUMAN,
Washington, D. C.:

At the moment when suffering mankind is standing on the threshold of a new and liberated world we receive with deep sorrow the news of the death of President Roosevelt. Through ceaseless labour he gave his life for the cause of humanity. May your Presidency be blessed in the continuation of his noble task.

HAAKON R.

❧

PALESTINE

JERUSALEM, *April 13, 1945.*

SECRETARY OF STATE,
Washington:

His Highness the Emir Abdullah has requested me to express to the Government and people of the United States his deep regret upon the death of President Roosevelt and to convey his personal sympathy to the President's family.

PINKERTON.

❧

PANAMA

PANAMA, *April 13, 1945.*

To His Excellency HARRY S. TRUMAN,
President of the United States of America,
Washington, D. C.:

Under the painful impression caused by the death of President Franklin D. Roosevelt, I wish to offer Your Excellency an expression of profound grief which this unhappy event has caused in my country. The Government and the people of Panama join the Government and people of the United States in the intense sorrow which overwhelms us all.

For the Republic of Panama, most particularly, the death of President Roosevelt constitutes an incalculable loss, he having been a tried and loyal friend, who carried out in practice the noble postulates of his exalted policy of the Good Neighbor.

In this hour, when the supreme exponent of human liberty and human dignity passes away from the scene, we cannot but offer up our prayers to the Almighty that He may inspire all men with the same energy, the same faith and the same nobility, so that with the great victory forged by his extraordinary and dynamic personality already in sight, the ideal of a better world may be realized.

Please accept, Excellency, with this expression of grief, the assurances of my highest and most distinguished consideration.

RICARDO ADOLFO DE LA GUARDIA,
President of the Republic of Panama.

PARAGUAY

ASUNCION, *April 13, 1945.*

His Excellency HARRY S. TRUMAN,
President of the United States of America,
Washington, D. C.:

With the painful impression caused by the unexpected death of the illustrious President and admired friend, Hon. Franklin D. Roosevelt, I express to Your Excellency the condolences of the Government and People of Paraguay. The passing of the greatest champion of democracy has filled with consternation my people who so honestly admired his vast and useful action in behalf of the highest and noblest ideals of humanity. The world, and especially America, loses in him the most enlightened leader in the crusade against the forces of aggression before his work could reach a triumphal end. Thanks to the firm and heroic determination of the glorious American people now under your leadership, that work, started by your illustrious predecessor will be continued.

HIGINIO MORINIGO,
President of the Republic of Paraguay.

PERU

LIMA, *April 13, 1945.*

Mrs. ELEANOR ROOSEVELT,
White House, Washington, D. C.:

I wish to convey to you and your children the sentiments of my deepest sympathy for the death of my great friend, President Roosevelt, whose loss constitutes an irreparable misfortune for the world and especially for the American nations, which always had full confidence in his exceptional capacity

and in the principles which he maintained during the long years of his administration to attain the highest degree of comprehension and mutual understanding among the peoples of this Hemisphere. With cordial salutations.

MANUEL PRADO.

PHILIPPINES

THE INN PONTEVEDRA FLO.
April 13.

The PRESIDENT,
  White House:

As the United States, together with the Philippines and the other liberty-
loving nations of the world, mourns the sudden passing of President Roosevelt, permit me, Mr. President to send to you on behalf of the Filipino peoples
the expression of our highest respect and confidence. I am doing this with
the firm conviction that the unfinished work of the departed President could
not have been entrusted to more safe and competent hands than yours. During this critical period in the history of the world, the free peoples will look to
you for inspiration and leadership, confident that the principles of total
victory, economic justice, and lasting peace which were so dear to the late
President, will find in you a new champion. May God continue to bestow
His blessings upon the great American Nation during your administration,
and may He assist you after victory is achieved to obtain for people everywhere liberty, peace, and security.

SERGIO OSMEÑA,
President of the Philippines.

POLAND

LONDON, April 13, 1945.

HARRY TRUMAN,
  President of the United States of America,
    White House, Washington, D. C.:

Please accept Mr. President, the assurance of the heartfelt sympathy of the
Polish Nation and myself with the American people in their grievous loss. In
President Roosevelt we shall mourn a great American and a great leader of the
United Nations who departed on the eve of the triumph of the cause in the

service of which he gave so much. At the moment when you are taking up the office of the highest executive of the United States of America I am sending you, Mr. President, my most sincere wishes for the success of your great and important mission. The approaching hour of victory will confront the United Nations with new gigantic problems of building up the postwar world, and I am sure that they will find in you a new defender of the ideals for which the freedom-loving nations of the world have been fighting for nearly six long years. The people of Poland trust that the secular traditions of common fighting for liberty will be continued under your leadership in this most difficult moment of our history.

WLADYSLAW RACZKIEWICZ,
President of the Republic of Poland.

PORTUGAL

BELEM, LISBOA, *April 13, 1945.*
To His Excellency The PRESIDENT OF THE UNITED STATES OF AMERICA,
Washington:

It is with deepest pain and sincerity that I present to Your Excellency in my name and that of the Portuguese people the expression of our heartfelt grief for the great loss suffered by your country and all the world in the person of the great statesman Franklin Delano Roosevelt.

GENERAL CARMONA,
President of the Portuguese Republic.

SAUDI ARABIA

Honorable EDWARD J. STETTINIUS,
Secretary of State,
Washington, D. C.:

In this hour I express the sorrow and consternation which have affected us so deeply for the loss of a great friend of his Majesty the King of Saudi Arabia the President Franklin Delano Roosevelt. I offer to the Government of the United States and to the American people the sympathies of the Government

FRANKLIN DELANO ROOSEVELT

of Saudi Arabia in this great loss which is not alone the loss of the United States but also of the whole world, especially in the circumstances of the present situation in which he was endeavouring to win for the world the principles of justice and righteousness.

YOUSUF YASIN,
Acting Foreign Minister.

❧

SPAIN

MADRID, *April 13, 1945.*

His Excellency HARRY S. TRUMAN,
 President of the United States, Washington, D. C.:

Accept, Excellency, the expression of my deepest sympathy for the great loss which the American people has suffered in the death of its illustrious President, Mr. Roosevelt.

FRANCISCO FRANCO,
Chief of the Spanish State.

❧   D - 4147

SWITZERLAND

BERN, *April 13, 1945.*

His Excellency HARRY TRUMAN,
 President of the United States of America,
  Washington, D. C.:

The unexpected death of His Excellency President F. D. Roosevelt, President of the United States, has caused throughout Switzerland the most profound emotion. The Federal Council and the Swiss people share with all their hearts in the sorrow felt by the American people which loses in President Roosevelt a great statesman.

STEIGER,
President of the Swiss Confederation.

(79)

FRANKLIN DELANO ROOSEVELT

SYRIA

SYRIAN LEGATION,
Washington, D. C., April 13, 1945.

The Honorable Mr. EDWARD R. STETTINIUS, Jr.,
Secretary of State, Washington, D. C.

SIR: Allow me to express to you, on behalf of the Government of Syria, my sincere condolences on the occasion of the untimely death of your great President, Franklin D. Roosevelt. The passing away of this great man and leader is a loss not to America alone, but to the whole of humanity. The Government and people of Syria, who have always been inspired by the principles for which he stood, are moved by deep sorrow and grief. They sincerely mourn the leader who showed such understanding of, and interest in, their cause and that of the whole Arab world. With his memory enshrined in their hearts and in the hearts of all peace loving peoples, they pray that the principles for which he sacrificed himself will prevail and that, in this way, the world will pay him the best and most fitting tribute.

Please accept, Sir, the renewed assurances of my highest consideration.

N. ROUOLS.

THAI

THE ROYAL THAI LEGATION,
Washington, D. C., April 13, 1945.

The Honorable EDWARD R. STETTINIUS, Jr.,
Secretary of State, Department of State,
Washington, D. C.

SIR: I have the honor to express to Your Excellency my most sincere and heartfelt condolences on the sudden and tragic death of His Excellency President Roosevelt. I feel sure that I am truly expressing the feelings of my people when I say that all Thais will find this bereavement almost as difficult to endure as the American people.

I would not presume to add my inadequate eulogies to the memory of a man who is assured of his place among the great benefactors of mankind. I would, however, venture to recall with the utmost gratitude that on the day follow-ing Pearl Harbor the President was gracious enough to include the following passage in his message to Congress:

"A little over a hundred years ago, in 1833, the United States entered into its first Far Eastern treaty, a treaty with Siam. It was a treaty providing for peace and for dependable relationships."

FRANKLIN DELANO ROOSEVELT

It is my firm hope and belief that when that peace, for which the late President labored so mightily, returns once more to the world, there will be a resumption of the former happy and dependable relationship between our two countries.

In conclusion, I would very much appreciate Your Excellency's good offices in conveying my deepest sympathies to Mrs. Roosevelt and to the members of her family.

I have the honor to be, Sir, with the highest consideration,

Your Excellency's obedient servant.

R. Seni Pramoj.

TURKEY

Ankara, *April 13, 1945.*

His Excellency Mr. Truman,
President of the United States of America,
Washington, D. C.:

The sudden death of President Roosevelt distressed me most profoundly. The entire Turkish nation joins me in view of this event which is as grievous as it is unexpected, coming at a moment when a world conference was preparing to submit to his great auspices the bases of the future organization of the peace. During my conferences in Cairo I had the opportunity of becoming acquainted personally with the eminent qualities, the humanitarian sentiment, and the absolute sincerity which permitted the illustrious deceased to serve not only our friend the American Nation but also the entire world, of which history will eternally keep a record of gratitude. Bowing before the grave of the great President, in my own name as well as in the name of the Turkish people, I share in the grief which has struck the United Nations so cruelly and beg Your Excellency to accept my most sorrowful condolences.

Ismet Inonu.

FRANKLIN DELANO ROOSEVELT

UNION OF SOUTH AFRICA

LEGATION OF THE UNION OF SOUTH AFRICA,
Washington, D. C., April 14, 1945.

The Honourable E. R. STETTINIUS, Jr.,
Secretary of State of the United States of America,
Department of State, Washington, D. C.

SIR: I have the honour to acknowledge the receipt of your letter of April 13 in which you announced the death of Franklin Delano Roosevelt, President of the United States of America, which occurred at Warm Springs, Georgia, at three thirty-five p. m. on April 12, 1945.

In accordance with your request, I have communicated the sad tidings to the Government of the Union of South Africa and have advised them that in obedience to the prescriptions of the Constitution, the office of President has devolved upon Harry S. Truman.

Accept, sir, the renewed assurances of my highest consideration.

JORDAAN.

UNION OF SOVIET SOCIALIST REPUBLICS

President TRUMAN,
Washington, D. C.:

In the name of the Soviet Government and in my personal behalf I express deep condolences to the Government of the United States of America on the untimely death of President Roosevelt. The American people and the United Nations have lost in the person of Franklin Roosevelt a great world statesman and the herald of world organization and security after the war. The Government of the Soviet Union expresses its deep sympathy to the American people in this heavy loss and its confidence that the policy of collaboration between the great powers engaged right now in the war against the common foe will continue to grow strong in the future.

J. STALIN.

FRANKLIN DELANO ROOSEVELT

URUGUAY

MONTEVIDEO, *April 13, 1945.*

Mr. HARRY S. TRUMAN,
   President of the United States,
      Washington, D. C.:

In the name of the Government of the Republic and my own, I offer you my sincere condolences for the death of the great democrat who presided over the destinies of the United States during the critical period since 1933. The figure of President Roosevelt as the constant defender of human dignity, as the founder and leader of the Good Neighbor policy, as the saviour of the democracies with Lend-Lease, and lastly as the untiring and firm backer of the admirable war effort of the United States, acquires enormous dimensions and all the freemen of the earth feel his loss as their own.

I avail myself of this opportunity to assure you of my highest consideration, and my best wishes for your personal happiness.

JUAN JOSÉ AMEZAGA,
President of the Oriental Republic of Uruguay.

VATICAN

CITADEL VATICANO.

To His Excellency the Honorable HARRY S. TRUMAN,
   President of the United States of America, Washington, D. C.:

The unexpected and sorrowful word of the passing of the President brings to our heart a profound sense of grief born of the high esteem in which we held this renowned statesman and of the friendly relations which he fostered and maintained with us and with the Holy See. To the expression of our condolences we join the assurance of our prayers for the entire American people and for their new President to whom we extend our fervent good wishes that his labors may be efficacious in leading the nations at war to an early peace that will be just and Christian.

PIUS PP XII.

FRANKLIN DELANO ROOSEVELT

VENEZUELA

MIRAFLORES, *April 13, 1945.*

Mrs. ELEANOR ROOSEVELT,
Washington, D. C.:

Mrs. Medina and I deeply regret the death of your illustrious husband, President Roosevelt, and extend to you and your children the sincere expression of our condolences.

ISAIAS MEDINA,
President of the United States of Venezuela.

YEMEN

The Very High PRESIDENCY OF THE UNITED STATES OF AMERICA:

I wish to express my deep and heartfelt sorrow as a result of the news of the death of the great President Mr. Franklin Roosevelt and I offer personally and in behalf of the people of my Kingdom sincere condolences to Your Exalted Excellency, to the honorable family of the late President, and the honorable American people. Please accept my sincere regards and deep respect.

AL-IMAM YAHYA,
King of Yemen.

YUGOSLAVIA

LONDON.

His Excellency PRESIDENT HARRY TRUMAN,
The White House, Washington, D. C.:

It is with the profoundest sense of loss that I learn of the sudden death of President Roosevelt. His magnificent understanding of world problems and untiring devotion to duty have been one of the greatest contributions to the inevitable outcome of the war. The staunch friendship he has always shown towards my country will never be forgotten by the Yugoslav Nation and myself. On assuming your high office I wish you every success in the task that lies before you.

PETER II R.

De Due